ACCESSING YOUR HIDDEN GREATNESS

by
Roberts Liardon

Unless otherwise indicated, all Scripture quotations are taken from the *King James Version* of the Bible.

Some quotations are taken from the *New King James Version* of the Bible. Copyright © 1979, 1980, 1982, by Thomas Nelson Inc., publishers.

1st Printing

Accessing Your Hidden Greatness
ISBN 1-890900-09-5

Copyright © 1999 by Roberts Liardon Ministries
P.O. Box 30710
Laguna Hills, CA 92654-0710

Published by Embassy Publishing Co.
P.O. Box 3500
Laguna Hills, CA 92654

Printed in the United States of America. All rights reserved under International Copyright Law. Contents and/or cover may not be reproduced in whole or in part in any form without the express written consent of the publisher.

Contents

1 Excellence Is A Choice...5

2 The Right Kind Of Insides...13

3 Daniel Was Not A Brown-Noser...............................17

4 The Triumphs & Troubles Of Divine Promotion...20

5 The Terrifying Price Of Treachery............................27

6 The Spiritual Disciplines Of Daniel..........................32

Chapter One

Excellence Is A Choice

Daniel is one of those men in the Bible I hope to live real close to in heaven. He intrigues me. God gave him supernatural knowledge and the ability to understand spiritual things. Because of his exceptional giftings, he became a ruler of people.

In Daniel 5:12 we read:

"Forasmuch as an excellent spirit, and knowledge, and understanding, interpreting of dreams, and shewing of hard sentences, and dissolving of doubts, were found in the same Daniel."

Why was Daniel full of supernatural understanding and knowledge? Why was he able to interpret dreams, explain hard sayings and dissolve doubts? It was because Daniel had an excellent spirit.

In a meeting one time, I watched those in the ministry of helps run up and down the aisles of the church. They were doing a great job getting water for the pastor and showing people to their seats. As I was sitting there minding my own business, the Lord spoke to me and said, *"Excellence of ministry they have, but no excellent spirit do they have!"*

It's good to have excellence of ministry, but we also need to have excellence of spirit.

Right Choices

An excellent spirit is not a gift, it is developed when you make right choices in life.

I often hear Christians say, "I want *the Lord* to be in charge of my life! I want *Him* to lead me." God does lead us, but sometimes Christians say things like that because they don't want to take the time to pray, read the Bible and make the right choices in life. They use spiritual terminology to create a religious camouflage for their own spiritual laziness.

Giftings, callings, and anointings are given to individuals who make right choices. Daniel made choices that pleased God and as the result, God protected Daniel all the days of his life.

There is a protection you can only find when you are obedient to God. You can pray, you can bind, you can loose, you can plead the blood; but God's protection will only be yours when you obey His Word with all your heart.

Choosing to live in truth is a protection for you. Truth is like a thick wall that surrounds your life and keeps evil from penetrating into your world. If there's evil in your life today, it's probably because you have not been living according to God's principles in certain areas.

Just because God is blessing you doesn't mean you're free to depart from God's principles either. You are responsible to live by divine principles even during times of great sovereign outpourings and revival.

If you'll grasp these truths and live according to them, God will place great anointings upon your life and grant you special powers to do wonders in the earth. But first, you must prove to God that you will be obedient to Him. God only promotes people who are obedient.

Some folks have a gift or special anointing, but God can't use them much because they think they can do anything they want. Well my friend, it just doesn't work that way. Everyone is required to be obedient and live according to God's principles. Everyone. Every prophet and every healer must choose in this day to be obedient to the Spirit and the Word.

Throughout my life and ministry, I have chosen to obey the Holy Spirit and God's Word. That's why sometimes I have found myself having dinner with very influential people. God knows He can trust me to say whatever He wants me to say. He also knows I will do whatever He tells me to do. If you choose to be obedient to the Holy Spirit and to make the right choices in life, God will do the same things through you.

Daniel Made Several Choices

Daniel made several choices that enabled him to develop an excellent spirit. The first is found in Daniel 1:8:

"Daniel purposed in his heart that he would not defile himself with the portion of the king's meat...."

In this particular story, Daniel would not eat the meat that came from the king's table because it was offered to idols. He would only eat those things which he knew were right in the sight of God.

How does this relate to us in our present day life? It means that we're not to allow the spirit of the world to taint us or the appetites of our flesh to dominate us. We must purpose in our heart to be a spiritual people in this natural earth. God brought Daniel into tender mercies and kept him from harm because Daniel refused to defile himself with the things of this fallen world.

The only way to overcome end-time trouble is to live in a manner that is pleasing to God. The perverse condition of our present society should not matter. As Christians, we live according to heaven's culture, not the world's. We can enjoy the natural places we live, but can't allow the perverted spirits of the territory to control our life-style.

Daniel stood in his day and said, "Even though I'm only a slave, even though I've been brought into captivity by powerful men of war, I'm not going to be defiled before my God in this heathen country full of idol worship."

Get the picture. At this point in history, the Israelites were a slave nation. They had been taken into captivity by the Babylonian Empire. Daniel was a slave. He had no rights to demand anything. They could have killed him for refusing to eat the king's meat. But you see, God protects those who stand upon right principles — He watches over those who purpose in their heart to do right. If you are determined not to defile yourself with sin and the lusts of this present world, God will make sure things turn out right for you.

Daniel Chose the Right Kind of Friends

In chapter 2 we see another choice that Daniel made — Daniel chose the right kind of friends.

In verse one, King Nebuchadnezzar has a troubling dream and he calls all his wise men, sorcerers, and wizards to interpret it. But they could not give him an answer. So the king became angry and decided to destroy all the wise men of Babylon.

Killing the wise men of Babylon wasn't such a bad idea. Most of the king's counselors were full of seducing devils anyway. Nevertheless, among the bad ones were four who had the right kind of inward grit. Their names were, Daniel, Meshach, Shadrach and Abed-Nego.

In verse 13 we read:

"the decree went forth that all the wise men should be slain, and they sought Daniel and his fellows to kill them."

Even though Daniel, Shadrach, Meshach, and Abed-Nego served the true and living God, they were considered to be among the false wise men. When Daniel heard about it, he marched right into the throne-room and said, "Hey! Hold on here king! Give me time to interpret the dream!"

Now that takes guts! You don't just go before a king and say, "Give me time!" Instead of chopping your head off, he may torture you to death! (If you're going to die, do it fast! Don't suffer!)

Because God was working in the situation, Nebuchadnezzar heeded Daniel and granted him extra time to interpret the dream. So Daniel took Shadrach, Meshach, and Abed-Nego to his house and they called on the Lord together.

Notice that Daniel chose the right kind of friends. If you're going to be the kind of person God can trust to carry great anointings, you've got to pick the right kinds of friends. You need friends who will pray with you and not just play golf with you.

In the end-times, your social life will be extremely important. I like friends. I have many of them around the world and I enjoy them, but all my friends can pray at the drop of a hat. There's not one of my close friends that I could not call at 3:30 in the morning and say, "I know you've been asleep, but I need some prayer right now. Would you pray?" They would jump out of bed, hit their knees, and they'd pray until they got a note of victory. These are the kind of friends you must surround yourself with. All the others, keep at the right distances. Don't let distant relationships disturb these kinds of valuable friendships in your life.

Daniel's friends knew how to pray. This is a very basic rule of close friendships. If they can't pray, they should not be close.

In my private conversations, I have been warning certain ones about the people they run with, but some of those I have spoken to are so dull that they don't hear me. One day they'll end up suffering, because they don't want to stop who they are running with.

While ministering at a conference in Russia, the Spirit of God came on me and gave me a word of prophecy for the pastor who was hosting the meeting. Under the unction of the Spirit, I warned the pastor to be careful on whom he leaned or he would have trouble in his camp. When I got done prophesying, the pastor took me behind the curtain and said, "Boy, you certainly read the mail of this church." The pastor was a good man, but he didn't know how to pick the right kinds of co-laborers. The devil got the wrong ones in there and almost split his great work.

Accessing Your Hidden Greatness

I'm warning you. In these last days, you had better pick the right kinds of friends. Divine relationships will be harder to hold on to than any other relationships you will have in your life. A golf buddy has no stress. The devil doesn't fight a little white ball that flies through the air! Pray for God to send you the right kind of friends and when they come, stick with them. ■

Chapter Two

The Right Kind Of Insides

*I*n Daniel chapter 3, we read another story about Daniel's three friends. When Daniel is promoted for accurately interpreting the king's dream, Shadrach, Meshach and Abed-Nego are promoted too. They helped Daniel pray down the interpretation of the dream from heaven and God rewarded them for it. God's promotion came to them because they had the right kind of insides.

In verse 1, Nebuchadnezzar decides to build a great statue of himself. Now that's called pride gone big time! The king thought, "Wow! I'm great! I'm it! I'll make a great image of myself and when the people hear the instruments and music, I will require them to bow down and worship me." Fortunately, there were three gutsy people in the kingdom who refused to bow. Their names were Shadrach, Meshach and Abed-Nego — the three close friends of the prophet Daniel.

When the guards saw that these three did not bow, they dragged them before King Nebuchadnezzar.

When Daniel's friends entered the throne-room, Nebuchadnezzar was seated upon his throne, holding his crown and scepter, surrounded by all his little "yes" men. In front of him stood a lady fanning him in the heat of the day and around him scurried a host of slaves tending to his every need.

"I was told by all the gossipers in the kingdom, that the three of you did not bow to my image," the king said, "I will now give you another chance to bow."

He could have given them five million chances and they still would not have bowed!

When you stand up for the principles of God, you never bow! Never, never, never! Why? Because truth will always prevail and bring great victory and freedom! If you bow, you will burn! What you compromise to get, you will lose somewhere down the road.

"I will have the music played again, and when the music plays, bow down to me and you will keep your life. If you do not bow, you will die."

Daniel's three friends stared brazenly at the king and said, "Oh Nebuchadnezzar, we are not careful to answer you in this manner! If it be so, our God whom we serve is able to deliver us from the burning fiery furnace. And He will deliver us out of thy hand, oh king, but if not, be it

The Right Kind Of Insides

known unto you, that we will not serve your gods, nor worship the golden image which you have set up for all men to bow down to!"

I love those words! "Let it be known! Our God is able to deliver us out of the burning fiery furnace, and out of your hand, oh king! We want you, and all your little puppets to know that we will *never* bow! If you heat the furnace seven times hotter, we still won't bow! We will burn and lose our life before we bow to you! There is only one true living God, and His name is Jehovah, and He can deliver us! But if He chooses not to, let it be known, we're still not going to bow!

These were the kinds of friends that Daniel had dinner with — that Daniel prayed with — that Daniel discussed spiritual matters and natural matters with. These were the kind of men that were close to Daniel's heart.

Who is close to your heart? Who knows the pattern of your heartbeat? Is it the right kind of friend, or is it one who is waiting for the right time to rip your heart to pieces? You must know who your friends are, my brother and sister. In this day and hour it's more important to know who you're running with than any other time in world history.

Shadrach, Meshach and Abed-Nego answered and said to the king, "Oh Nebuchadnezzar, we are not careful..." That means that they were not nervous about the stand they were taking. They didn't have to think twice or take a vote. They knew *exactly* what they were going to say and all three of them said the same thing. Now that's unusual.

"Our God is able to deliver us," they declared, "but if He does not, we will die in the fiery furnace and we will go to our eternal reward in heaven!"

If you want God to trust you, anoint and promote you, you must walk with the right kinds of people. Your friends will influence your public and private actions. Before God grants you certain types of power, He must make sure that you will carry it right. He must know that you will not allow the gift and anointing to be endangered, misused or merchandised.

Those who you run with must have a respect for the anointing upon your life. Many great men have paid a private price for their anointing, but have allowed their friends to merchandise what God has granted supernaturally. Your friends must understand how God has called you. You must understand how God has called them too, and you must respect each other; never biting, cheating or misappropriating the anointings God has entrusted to you.

It's important that Christians learn how to relate to one another in these last days. Not everyone has the same gift or anointing, but you can still run together if you learn how to discern and respect each other's God-given role. ■

Chapter Three

Daniel Was Not A "Brown-Noser"

*I*n Daniel chapter 6 we have another great story about the character of Daniel. Daniel was not a "brown-noser." He obeyed God and God promoted him. In verse 1 we read:

"It pleased Darius to set over the kingdom one hundred and twenty satraps, to be over the whole kingdom; and over these, three governors, of whom Daniel was one, that the satraps might give account to them, so that the king would suffer no loss. Then this Daniel distinguished himself above the governors and satraps, because an excellent spirit was in him; and the king gave thought to setting him over the whole realm."

Dan 6:1-3 (NKJ)

Here Daniel faces another crazy king. I don't know why, but it seems to me that most natural leaders have no sense. They compromise to get into office and then lie to remain in office. Thank God that in the kingdom, we don't have to do either one. We just obey and we are honored for doing what is right in the sight of God.

God alone holds the power of promotion. You do not need to cater to anyone. Just obey the Word and the heavenly call and promotion will come from the Lord. In these times it's important to understand that "Promotion does not come from the east or the west, but it comes from the Lord." (Ps 75:6)

God is the one who exalts one and brings down another. You don't need to brown-nose your way into something. All you need to do is obey the Lord.

Promotion comes from above, my friend. It doesn't come by seeking those who seem to have power and money. When God promotes, no man can take it away. When the Holy One sets it up, it remains forever.

So we see in chapter 6 that Daniel was promoted to be one of three governors over the entire kingdom. He began as a Jewish slave from a foreign country and ended up seated at the right hand of all the movements of power. He knew the money, he knew the law, he knew what was going on — he was promoted by God into the highest echelon of influence within the kingdom. He was almost what we would consider a vice president.

Daniel's job was to watch over the king so that he would "suffer no damage..." In other words, Daniel was to keep the king from being "ripped off."

Daniel Was Not a "Brown-Noser"

Verse 3 says:

"Then this Daniel distinguished himself above the governors and satraps, because an excellent spirit was in him; and the king gave thought to setting him over the whole realm."

This means that Daniel was trustable. There was no conniving in him. He was not concealing another agenda. The king felt safe around him.

Sometimes, when I walk up to people, I feel something mysterious — like something is up — like there is a hidden agenda lurking just underneath the surface. There was none of that in Daniel. He had an excellent and forthright spirit. He didn't hide, or connive — he was clean, honest and up front.

Sometimes people walk up to me and say, "I'm planning a great work for God and I want you to help me." Believe me, I'd love to help, but sometimes I can't because their inward parts aren't right. There's a hidden agenda being formed there. The Holy Spirit forewarns people in leadership so that these types of agendas do not pervert and destroy the ultimate plan of God.

You must be like Daniel and develop an excellent spirit. You must be one whose agenda can be investigated and no fault will be found. ■

Chapter Four

The Triumphs & Troubles Of Divine Promotion

In Daniel chapter 6 we see some of the troubles Daniel faced when he moved into his season of divine promotion. In verses 4-9 we read:

"So the governors and satraps sought to find some charge against Daniel concerning the kingdom; but they could find no charge or fault, because he was faithful; nor was there any error or fault found in him. Then these men said, 'We shall not find any charge against this Daniel unless we find it against him concerning the law of his God.' So these governors and satraps thronged before the king, and said thus to him: 'King Darius, live forever! All the governors of the kingdom, the administrators and satraps, the counselors and advisors, have consulted together to establish a royal statute and to make a firm decree, that whoever petitions any god or man for thirty days, except you, O king, shall be cast into the den of lions. Now, O king, establish the decree and sign the writing, so that it cannot be changed, according to the law of the

The Triumphs & Troubles Of Divine Promotion

Medes and Persians, which does not alter.' Therefore King Darius signed the written decree."

Dan 6:4-9 (NKJ)

Because Daniel was promoted, those around about him got upset. They tried to find fault so they could accuse him and get him out of power. But, they could find nothing of which to accuse Daniel. There was no loss of money, there was no mismanagement of the king's goods, nothing. Everything was in perfect order. So those around Daniel made up a new law and suggested it to the king in order to get Daniel out of their way.

"Oh king, there is none like you," they said, "make a law that there shall be worshipping of no other god but you."

It's amazing how many times God will intervene when flattering lips put great men into jeopardy. These jealous rulers knew that the only place they could get Daniel was in his steadfastness toward God. They saw that it was how Daniel lived a protected life.

Protection doesn't come by guns or armies, my friend, it comes by living right in the sight of God! Did you get that? It doesn't matter if you're in a Los Angeles gang riot! If you're doing what is right in the sight of God, God will protect you!

These wicked men waited to see if Daniel was going to disobey a natural law to uphold a spiritual law. Natural laws should never cause you to disobey spiritual laws. If you have to decide which one to obey, go with the higher law. If you uphold the higher law, God will move to defend and protect you.

In verse 10 the story continues:

"Now when Daniel knew that the writing was signed, he went home. And in his upper room, with his windows open toward Jerusalem, he knelt down on his knees three times that day, and prayed and gave thanks before his God, as was his custom since early days."

Dan 6:10 (NKJ)

This shows that Daniel was a man of prayer. He wasn't praying because there was a crisis in the land. It was his custom to pray three times a day. That's why he was great — that's why God could trust him and reveal to him things pertaining to our time today. God showed Daniel things that would happen thousands of years in advance. Before our great grandparents were even born, God pulled back the screen and said, "Daniel, behold the future, and what shall take place." God will only show these kinds of things to those He trusts. God knew Daniel's insides. God trusted Daniel because, He heard from Daniel regularly. Daniel's voice came up to God's throne three times a day with supplications, prayers, questions and intercessions. God knew the attitude of Daniel's heart by Daniel's many questions and prayers, thus God could trust him.

Despite the king's decree, Daniel continued to pray three times a day. He was not afraid of anything or anyone because he knew God would protect him. Daniel opened his window, turned toward Jerusalem and began to pray. Then those whose mouth's were full of flattery moved in for the kill. They ran to the king and said, "Hey, we caught Daniel praying!"

I wish the king could have been a little more discerning. I wish he could have seen that those around him had executed an evil plan to remove this righteous man from power.

There are evil agendas today working throughout the nations of the world to remove righteous men and women from power! There are evil agendas trying to remove churches from their divine positions! But God will deliver those who have an excellent spirit and the upright shall remain!

So these wicked rulers said to the king, "Daniel has not done what you have decreed! You've said if they don't do what you say, they must be thrown in the den of lions!"

A den of lions had been prepared for the criminals of the kingdom. Humans were their meal. These lions were deprived of food so when they threw a human in there, the human would not live long. It was the king's way of punishing all who disobeyed the laws of the land.

It is important to obey the laws of the land, but we must not forget that the law of God exceeds every natural law. It's good when the laws of the earth agree with the laws of heaven, but many times, even in our nation today, these laws are contrary to one another. That's why those of us who try to live right in the sight of God are looked at as a resistant people — a people who do not want progression. We do want progression, but what most people today call progression is really deterioration.

So the king was upset with himself for making the decree. He worked all day long to see if there was a way he could deliver Daniel, his most favored servant. But according to the law of the Medes and Persians, there was nothing that could be done to the change the decree. With great heaviness of heart, the king commanded that Daniel be cast into the den of lions.

"Your God, whom you serve continually, He will deliver you," said the king as the guards dragged Daniel away.

Daniel lived so good, that he had even convinced the king that his God was a deliverer! Hallelujah!

Your actions and deeds will be read by them who watch you. It goes back to the old standard that says: "Your life is the greatest sermon you'll ever preach."

"Then a stone was brought and laid on the mouth of the den, and the king sealed it with his own signet ring and with the signets of his lords, that the purpose concerning Daniel might not be changed. Now the king went to his palace and spent the night fasting; and no musicians were brought before him. Also his sleep went from him."

The Triumphs & Troubles Of Divine Promotion

Dan 6:17-18 (NKJ)

The king paced through the palace corridors waiting for morning to see if Daniel's God had delivered him. The king was grieved at the thought of loosing Daniel because Daniel had an excellent spirit and he was trustable.

(The world and even wicked leaders search for those who have an excellent spirit to stand beside them — they want to be surrounded with people they can trust.)

The king's reign was in trouble. The king knew that if Daniel was to die, the other treacherous men would take power. Those who have an excellent spirit are loyal. They keep things in order. You can trust them to use their great ability to defend and protect you.

As the sun broke across the hills the following morning, the king ran to where the den was and moved away the stone.

"Servant of the living God," cried the king, "has your God whom you serve continually delivered you from the lions? "

"Oh king, live forever!" Daniel responded.

What sweet sounds to the king's ears! The servant whom he loved so much answered and said, "Live forever!"

The king knew he would be safe now too, because Daniel was alive. The wicked ones around him would no longer be able to take his reign. The king was confident

Accessing Your Hidden Greatness

that Daniel would protect him because Daniel was a man who had an excellent spirit!

Daniel said to the king, "My God sent an angel, and shut the mouths of the lions, and they have not hurt me. Forasmuch as before Him, innocence was found in me! I have done you no wrong, oh king! I have not stolen money, I have not mismanaged your goods. I have wronged no one, even when they have wronged me! I have done what is right in the sight of God, and in your sight too, oh king!"

The king was exceedingly glad for Daniel and commanded that they should draw Daniel up out of the den. When Daniel stood before the king, no manner of hurt could be found upon him. Why was that? It was because he believed in his God! ■

Chapter Five

The Terrifying Price Of Treachery

God turned the tables on those who sought to destroy Daniel. In verse 24 of chapter 6 we read:

"...the king gave the command, and they brought those men who had accused Daniel, and they cast them into the den of lions — them, their children, and their wives; and the lions overpowered them, and broke all their bones in pieces before they ever came to the bottom of the den."

Dan 6:24 (NKJ)

I tell you it doesn't pay to do wrong! It doesn't pay to touch God's anointed! It doesn't pay to be mischievous, envious and jealous! It does not pay my brother and sister!

While Daniel was in the lion's den, the wicked rulers threw a party. They enjoyed a few moments of power. They probably thought, "We got rid of the man that stood in our way! Now we can rule! Now our agenda can dominate and the king will do what we say!"

The Terrifying Price Of Treachery

But Daniel was alive! He lived because he served the only true and living God! A dead god can't deliver you, only a living one can! Because of Daniel's faithfulness, God reached down and supernaturally shut the mouth of those starving lions! It was no wonder these wicked rulers were broken to pieces before they hit the bottom of the cave. The lions had been starving for days, plus Daniel had been down there walking around in front of them! They wanted to eat Daniel but the living God had shut their mouths!

If you're reading this book and your agenda is not right, it would be wise for you to fall on your face and cry out to God right now! You don't know when your day of judgment will come!

There is a day when we'll all be judged, but there are also little judgment days throughout our lives. There are days when God says, "Enough is enough! You've crossed the line and I will no longer allow you to continue to do what you're doing!"

New Testament Judgments

Don't think that because you're under grace, judgment does not exist. Judgment does fall during this time of grace. Just look at the New Testament. Just look at Ananias and Sapphira. They were in the early church — they saw the power — they knew Peter was a great apostle and that he had connections above. You don't lie

The Terrifying Price Of Treachery

to the Holy Ghost my friend. You just don't do it. When judgment came, Ananias fell first and the young men in the church had to take him out and bury him. His wife came in next and before the young men could even get a drink of water, they had to bury her too! It's amazing what kind of jobs God will give the young men in the church!

There *is* judgment within the New Testament church. It may be prolonged because of God's grace and mercy, but God will always bring things into check and balance. God's judgment is a part of His mercy. God is being merciful to His people when He exposes the hidden agendas of wicked individuals within the church.

When God's decree of judgement comes, if you are not right — if you have not repented — it will be a time of great sorrow. There will be trouble in your life and it will be your own fault. You may even cry out to God and say, "Why is this happening to me?" And He'll respond, "You've brought it on your own head!"

There are many who do whatever they want in the name of God, but judgment day is coming! Before the great white throne judgment, another judgment will come! God judges some things right here and now.

Why do some Christians suffer so much? It's not always because the devil is fighting them! Sometimes it's because they have continued to willfully disobey God. When you continue down a road of wrongdoing, what's at the end of that road will one day come into your life. It's not worth it, my friend! It's just not worth it!

We will all one day face the great white throne judgment, but we must never forget that there are little days of judgment that come throughout our life.

If you're not right with God or if you're not right with your fellow man, it would be wise for you to get things straight before the sun goes down today.

When God brings His judgment into the earth, those who are doing wrong are put right. Every ill-gotten gain will be lost and every position attained by wrong motives and political maneuverings will be gone. In one day it will all disappear. You've got to get where you're going by doing what is right. You cannot get there by doing wrong.

The men who were jealous of Daniel tried to take power through deceit. They wanted to be an influential force over the king. They hated Daniel because Daniel told the truth and did what was right in the sight of God and the king. Twenty four hours later, these mischievous men were thrown into the lion's den along with their wives and their children.

This is sad but true; if the head of the house does wrong, the whole house will suffer. I wish there was some way we could stop it from happening, but it's in the Bible. When the head of the house does wrong, it comes upon the wife and the children. It is sometimes passed on to other generations as well.

The Terrifying Price Of Treachery

If you're in positions now because of wrong motives or if you're not doing what is right, it would be wise to set things in order before the judgment of God falls unexpectedly upon your life. When the day of judgment comes, everything that you've gained by wrongdoing will be lost. Every power that you illegally hold will be gone. Every bit of false prestige will be lost forever. You'll find yourself with nothing. You'll feel like you've lost all your money and your importance. It will be your own fault because you got it the wrong way. These men died because of selfish ambition. Their wives suffered and their kids suffered too. Their kids didn't even have a chance to begin their lives! They died because of the wickedness of their fathers! ■

Chapter Six

The Spiritual Disciplines of Daniel

In Daniel chapter 7, we find that Daniel was a man of great spiritual discipline. He had the ability to keep things in his spirit until the proper time. In verse 28, Daniel makes an interesting statement. He says:

"...but I kept the matter in my heart."

Oh how I wish men would learn how to hold things until the proper time of release!

I was ministering to a church in the Carolinas one time when the pastor began to announce certain things to his congregation. In my spirit, I knew that this pastor was saying things before their proper time. The pastor ended up causing unnecessary conflict and war because he could not keep things until the right time of release.

There are many things that God would share with you if you would only learn to hold the words of your mouth.

Daniel Was A Student Of The Word

In Daniel the 9th chapter, we see another spiritual discipline in Daniel's life. In the 2nd verse, we read:

"...I, Daniel, understood by the books, the number of years where of the Word of the Lord came by Jeremiah the prophet. That He would accomplish the seventy years in the desolations of Jerusalem."

Notice Daniel says, "I understood by the books." That meant he studied the books. That meant he opened up the scriptures and he studied them. Daniel did not just sit around trying to see a vision. He was a student of the scriptures — he studied the prophet's words.

If our generation would study the Bible more, there would come great outbreaks of God's refreshing and God's power. If Christians would stop studying end-time paranoia and begin studying their end-time duties, there would be much more activity. Most Christians have not studied the Book for themselves. They have relied on men's ideas about the scriptures. It's time to go back to the Book. It's time for us to know what the Book says for ourselves. Daniel understood things pertaining to his time as well as ours because he was a student of the scriptures.

Fasting And Prayer

Chapter 10 is my favorite chapter pertaining to the life of Daniel. In verse 3, we see that Daniel had been fasting and praying for 21 days.

Some folks can't fast and pray for 21 minutes! No wonder there's so much trouble in their families! No wonder there is so much unnecessary warfare!

After fasting and praying for 21 days, Daniel learned a great lesson. He found out that prayers are sometimes hindered by demon princes that live over territories. Principalities and powers battle viciously to stop truth, because they know that one word from heaven can change a course of a nation. They understand that one word from heaven can change the course of the entire planet. That is why demon powers fight so hard to keep from you hearing the voice of God. That is why they do their best to keep you from knowing what the Bible has to say about your life.

The devil works hard to make sure there is trouble, static and distraction when you try to read the Bible and pray. He wants to make sure you don't hear from God clearly. He doesn't want you to have end-time understanding. He wants to make sure you don't find out what is written about you in the Bible.

Last Days Adventures

The Spirit of God is looking throughout the earth for those who have a humble heart and an excellent spirit. You'll be amazed when you see who God chooses to lead the next move. They will come from where no one would think. They may not dress just right, and they may not talk just right, but the Lord will be upon them because they were able to hear from heaven and press through.

Those who have nothing to gain or protect in the natural will get more from God than those who are always trying to defend what little they've got. Throughout the Bible, and throughout church history, God finds men and women with a humble heart and an excellent spirit. Who would have ever thought that an uneducated hill-billy from Kentucky named William Branham would become the number one prophet of his day? Who would have thought that a red headed woman named Kathryn Kuhlman from Concordia, Missouri, would be the leading revivalist of her time? Who would have ever thought that a woman from Canada named Aimee Semple McPherson would become the spiritual governor of Los Angeles? You'd think that God would choose somebody with degrees, money, and political connections, but who does God choose instead? Those who have no agendas — those who are not trying to protect something that God didn't give them. He uses those who are not pursuing something that God doesn't want them to have. God is looking for folks who will just say, "Lord, whatever."

Daniel probably never knew that he would become one of the major ruling powers of a foreign nation. He never became the king, but he was up there in the palace workings. He was right in the middle of the king's discussions. Who did they ask to interpret dreams? Who brought the Word of the Lord when the hand of God wrote the script on the wall? It was Daniel.

Last-days adventures are for those who lose their lives and go the way God wants them to go. They are for those who live right and make right choices in life. They are for those who have an excellent spirit.

There are many reading this book who are in a season of development. At the right time, God will pull back the curtain and place you on the stage of your divine destiny. But right now, you are still in a time of preparation. Don't despise the season you're in and don't treat God's dealings lightly.

Those who have the greatest call are often the ones who have the dullest hearing. God is trying to get your attention today! He is trying to prepare your insides so that when you finally step onto the platform of your destiny, you won't fall flat on your face! God is working. If you'll give ear to Him, your future will be bright and all will be well! ■

Spirit Life Partner

Roberts Liardon

Wouldn't It Be Great...

- If you could feed over 1,000 hungry people every week?
- If you could travel 250,000 air miles, boldly preaching the Word of God in 94 nations?
- If you could strengthen and train the next generation of God's leaders?
- If you could translate 31 books and distribute them into 47 languages?

...Now You Can!

Maybe you can't go, but by supporting this ministry every month, your gift can help to communicate the gospel around the world.

SLBC graduates ministering in the Philippines–provided by Spirit Life Partners world-wide. Thank you for your ongoing support!

CLIP ALONG LINE & MAIL TO ROBERTS LIARDON MINISTRIES.

☐ **YES!!** Pastor Roberts, I want to support your work in the kingdom of God by becoming a **SPIRIT LIFE PARTNER**. Please find enclosed my first monthly gift.

Name_____
Address_____
City_____ State _____ Zip _____
Phone ( ) _____ Email_____

SPIRIT LIFE PARTNER AMOUNT: $ _____

☐ Check / Money Order ☐ VISA ☐ American Express ☐ Discover ☐ MasterCard

☐☐☐☐ ☐☐☐☐ ☐☐☐☐ ☐☐☐☐

Name On Card_____ Exp. Date __/__

Signature_____ Date __/__

Roberts Liardon Ministries

P.O. Box 30710 ♦ Laguna Hills, CA 92654 USA ♦ (949) 833-3555 ♦ Fax (949) 833.9555 ♦ www.robertsliardon.org

BOOKS
by Roberts Liardon

A Call To Action
Accessing Your Hidden Greatness
Almost Christian: Exposing the Two-Faced Believer
Breaking Controlling Powers:
(A Compilation of 3 Bestselling Books)
Cry of the Spirit
Don't Let the Devil Destroy Your Purpose
Extremists, Radicals and Non-Conformists
Final Approach
Forget Not His Benefits
God's Generals
Greater, Wiser, Stronger
Haunted Houses, Ghosts and Demons
How To Get Your Spirit In Shape and Keep It
How to Stay In Your High Calling and Not Come Out!
I Saw Heaven
Kathryn Kuhlman
Knowing People by the Spirit
On Her Knees
Religious Politics
School of the Spirit
Sharpening Your Discernment
Smith Wigglesworth - Complete Collection
Smith Wigglesworth Speaks to Students
The Most Dangerous Place To Be
The Spirit of Reformation: You Can Change The World
3rd Degree Burn
Three Outs and You're In
Why The Devil Doesn't Want You To Pray In Tongues
You Can Jumpstart Your Gift

To place an order call: (949) 833-3555
or visit our website at: www.robertsliardon.org

Seven reasons you should attend Spirit Life Bible College

1. SLBC is a **spiritual school** with an academic support; not an academic school with a spiritual touch.

2. SLBC teachers are **successful ministers** in their own right. Pastor Roberts Liardon will not allow failure to be imparted into his students.

3. SLBC is a member of **Oral Roberts University Educational Fellowship** and is **fully accredited** by the International Christian Accreditation Association.

4. SLBC hosts monthly seminars with some of the **world's greatest** ministers who add another element, anointing and impartation to the students' lives.

5. Roberts Liardon understands your commitment to come to SLBC and commits himself to students by **ministering weekly** in classroom settings.

6. SLBC provides **hands-on** ministerial training.

7. SLBC provides ministry opportunity through its **post-graduate placement program**.

---------------------- CLIP ALONG LINE & MAIL TO ROBERTS LIARDON MINISTRIES. ----------------------

☐ **YES!** Pastor Roberts, please rush me a **FREE VIDEO** and information packet for **SPIRIT LIFE BIBLE COLLEGE**.

Name_____

Address_____

City_____ State _____ Zip _____

Phone ( )_____ Email_____

Roberts Liardon Ministries
P.O. Box 30710 ♦ Laguna Hills, CA 92654-0710
(949) 833.3555 ♦ Fax (949) 833.9555
www.robertsliardon.org

We do not discriminate regardless of race, color, national origin, sex, or age.

ROBERTS LIARDON MINISTRIES INTERNATIONAL OFFICES

USA
Roberts Liardon Ministries
P.O. Box 30710
Laguna Hills, CA 92654-0710
(949) 833-3555

EUROPE
Roberts Liardon Ministries
P.O. Box 295
Welwyn Garden City
AL7 2ZG
England
011-44-1707-327-222

SOUTH AFRICA
Roberts Liardon Ministries
P.O. Box 3155
Kimberely 8300
South Africa
011-27-53-832-1207

PHILIPPINES
Roberts Liardon Ministries
P.O. Box 154
Ilollo City 5000
(6333) 329-4537
Email: rlm-phil@iloilo.net

Visit us on the WorldWide Web at:
www.robertsliardon.org